Guthrie.

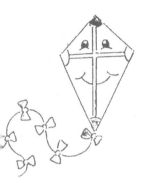

To Parents

About this word book

The *Parent and Child First Word Book* is a fun and practical way to introduce your child to letter sounds and letter shapes. For each letter there is a picture of a lively scene illustrating a selection of words that begin with that letter, plus a selection of these pulled out and labelled around the outside.

The composite pictures will help your child to become confident at hearing and recognizing the sounds of letters of the alphabet. Where a letter has more than one sound, the small labelled pictures include only words that begin with the sound your child will learn first at school. For example, the pages illustrating the letter "**a**" include words like **apple** and **acrobat** (which begin with a short "a" sound). Words that begin with a different "a" sound, like **accordion**, are included only in the main scene. When you use these pages with your young child, refer to the sound that is illustrated and help your child to point out the things that begin with that sound. There are many more examples for your child to find in the main picture in addition to the ones labelled around the outside.

Helping your child

▷ When your child starts to attempt his or her own writing you will find the *First Word Book* a very useful first spelling aid. It can be used for stories, poems, scrapbooks, letters, notices, cards, lists and to complement the activities in the other books in *The Parent and Child Programme.*

▷ Keep the *First Word Book* somewhere at hand — as your child becomes more interested in words and spellings, you'll find it useful to refer to on all sorts of occasions.

▷ Concentrate on one particular letter sound at a time. Ask your child to describe what is going on in the main picture.

▷ See if your child can find all the items labelled in the small pictures in the main picture. Helping children *to look carefully* encourages important early reading skills.

▷ Emphasize the first *letter sound* of all the labelled words then ask your child if he or she can point out more things beginning with this sound in the main picture. Learning letter sounds is another important part of learning to read.

▷ Look for things in your home beginning with a particular letter or play a game of I-spy. Don't go on for too long, though, or try to correct your child. Always praise your child's good guesses.

▷ Learning to recognize the shapes of the individual letters is important, too. Use the alphabet at the top of each page to point out the coloured letter. You could look for other examples of a particular letter — when you are out shopping or in the kitchen together, for example.

▷ Again, only do one letter at a time. Young children can't concentrate for long so don't go on if your child is losing interest or becoming tired!

First Word Book

Educational adviser
Jane Salt
Advisory Teacher for the Early Years, Merton

This book belongs to

Illustrated by
Kate Jaspers

a b c d e f g h i j k l m

apple

acrobat

animal

ankle

alligator

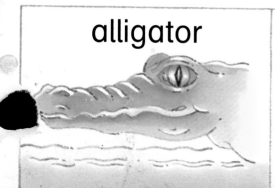

axe

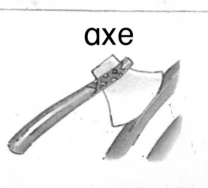

n o p q r s t u v w x y z

astronaut

admiral

ant

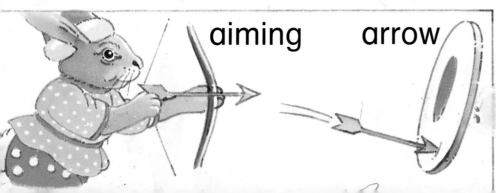

aiming   arrow

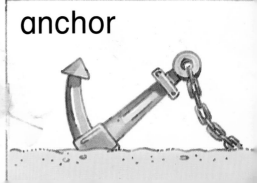

anchor

a b c d e f g h i j k l m

bath

ball

book

bird

bucket

balloon

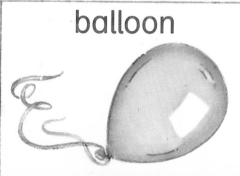

bottle

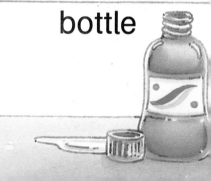

n o p q r s t u v w x y z

banging

beak

boat

bursting

button

bubble

bear

a b c d e f g h i j k l m

café

camera

cobweb

caravan

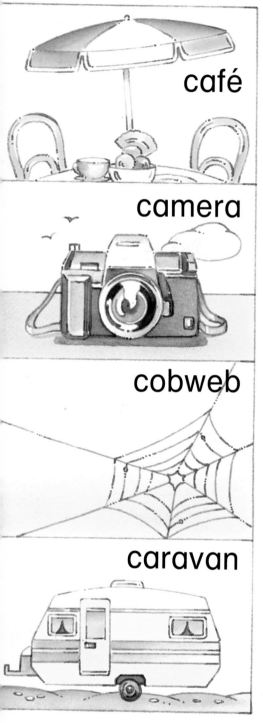

counting

car

comic

n o p q r s t u v w x y z

castle

cow

cake

cat

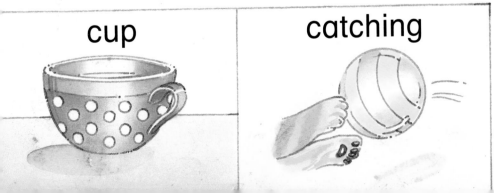

cup

catching

cave

a b c d e f g h i j k l m

dog

dirt

duck

ditch

door

diving

dish

n o p q r s t u v w x y z

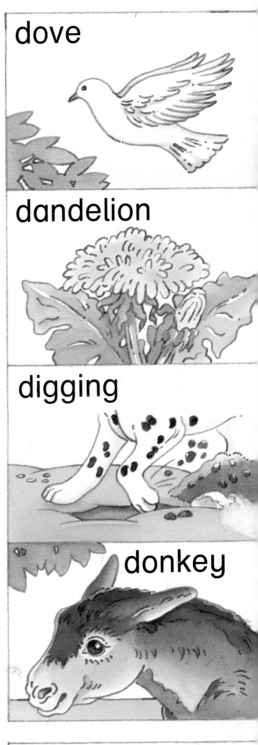

dove

dandelion

digging

donkey

daffodil

deer

daisy

a b c d e f g h i j k l m

elephant

elbow

exit

explorer

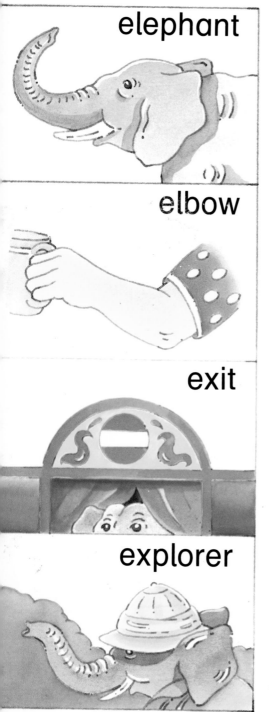

engine

exploring

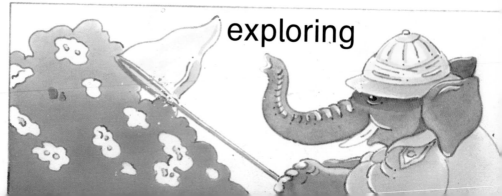

n o p q r s t u v w x y z

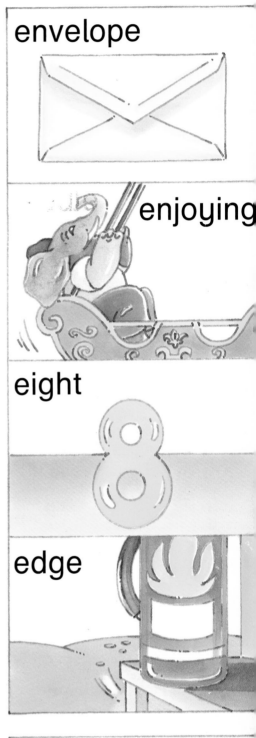

envelope

enjoying

eight

edge

entrance

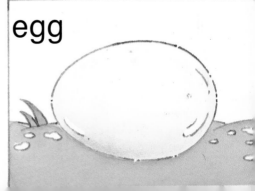

egg

a b c d e f g h i j k l m

fox

face

fighting

frog

foal

fire

feather

n o p q r s t u v w x y z

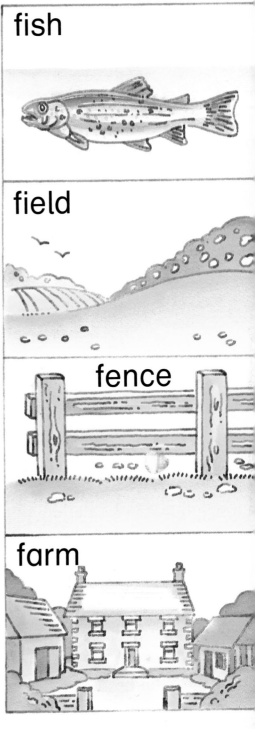

fish

field

fence

farm

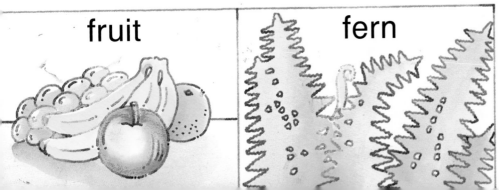

fruit

fern

fishing

a b c d e f g h i j k l m

goldfish

garage

garden

guitar

giggling

game

goat

n o p q r s t u v w x y z

gorilla

guard

geese

goggles

gate

gift

giving

a b c d e f g h i j k l m

hippo

hill

head

house

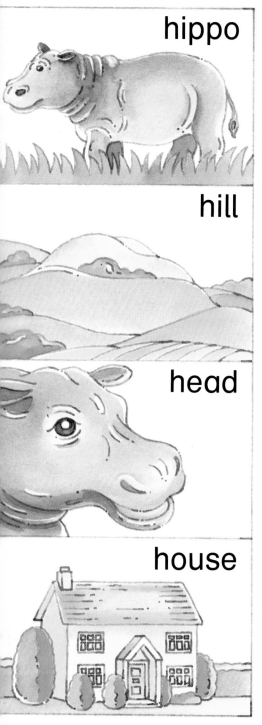

hosepipe

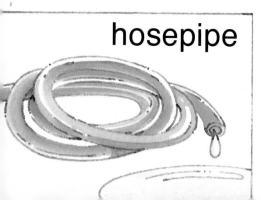

hut

hook

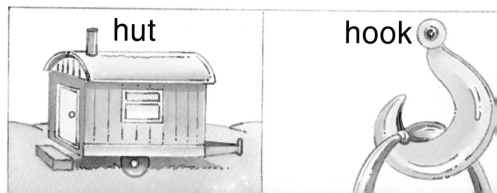

n o p q r s t u v w x y z

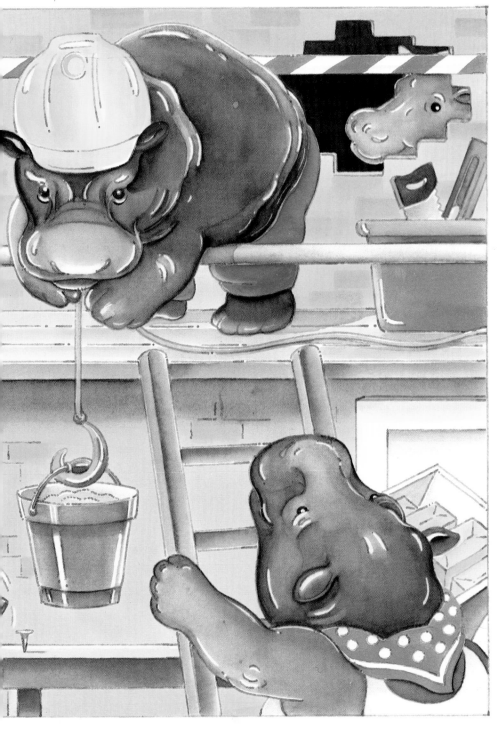

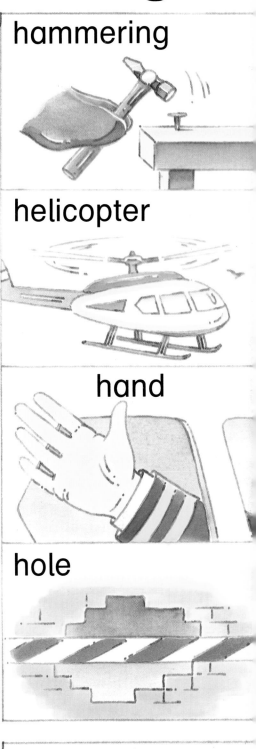

hammering

helicopter

hand

hole

helmet

hammer

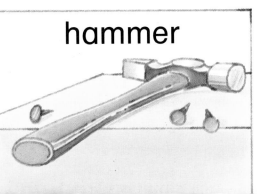

holding

a b c d e f g h i j k l m

insect

juice

jug

jelly

jacket

jumping

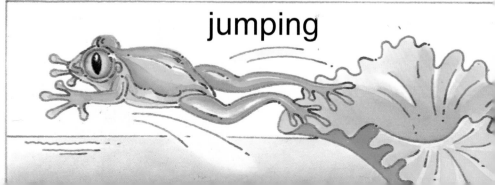

n o p q r s t u v w x y z

invitation

juggling

instrument

jewelry

ill

igloo

a b c d e f g h i j k l m

kangaroo

kicking

kettle

kite

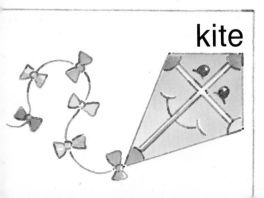

koala

kitten

n o p q r s t u v w x y z

kingfisher

keyhole

key

kilt

kissing

king

a b c d e f g h i j k l m

leopard

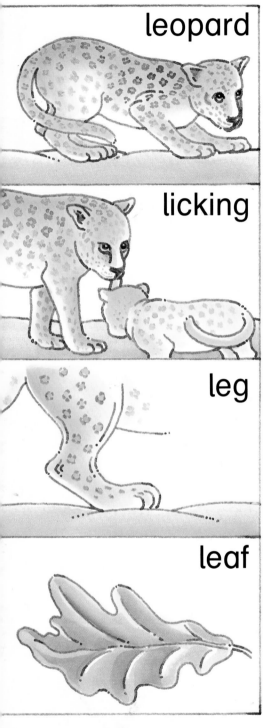

licking

leg

leaf

light

lizard

log

n o p q r s t u v w x y z

lamb

ladybird

lake

litter

lion

lying

ladder

a b c d e f g h i j k l m

mushroom

mat

melon

mug

milk

meat

mask

n o p q r s t u v w x y z

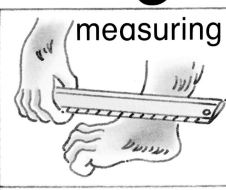
measuring

meeting

monkey

mirror
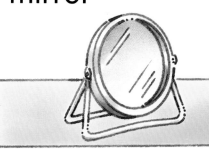

money
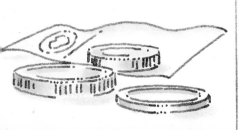

mouth

magazine

a b c d e f g h i j k l m

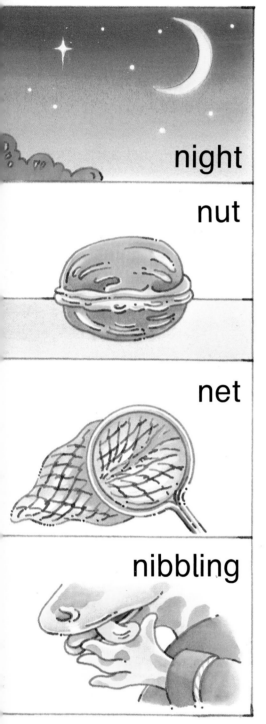

night

nut

net

nibbling

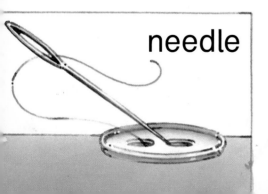

needle

necklace

nail

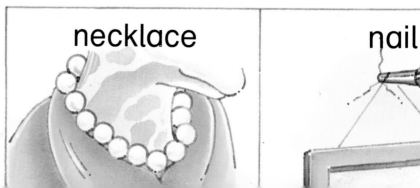

n o p q r s t u v w x y z

nudging

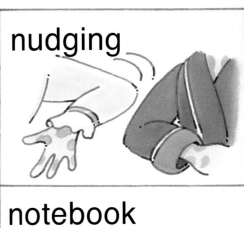
notebook

nose

nine

nightdress

nib

newspaper

a b c d e f g h i j k l m

owl

panda

parrot

pond

ostrich

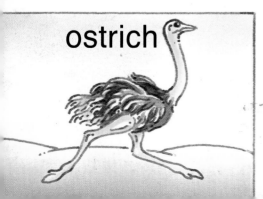

pig

pony

n o p q r s t u v w x y z

pizza

otter

pushing

orange

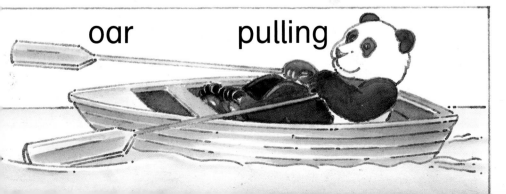

oar   pulling

penguin

a b c d e f g h i j k l m

rabbit

queen

reading

quarrelling

robot

rug

radio

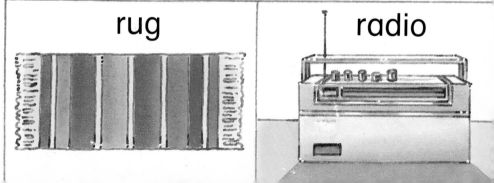

n o p q r s t u v w x y z

quilt

rose

quarter

ribbon

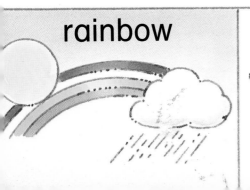

rainbow

rocket

rollerskate

a b c d e f g h i j k l m

sun

sea

sailing

seagull

sail

sausage

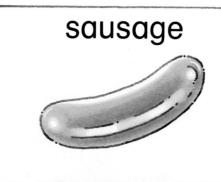

sandwich

n o p q r s t u v w x y z

sandcastle

sand

seal

sitting

sock

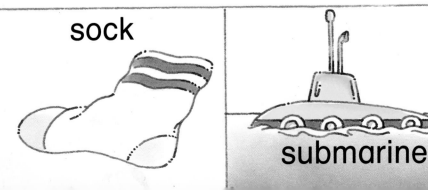

submarine

seaweed

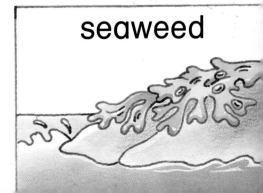

a b c d e f g h i j k l m

tortoise

talking

table

ticket

telephone

teddy

television

n o p q r s **t** u v w x y z

tiger

tooth

tail

tapping

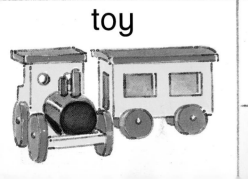

toy

teapot

tunnel

a b c d e f g h i j k l m

vulture

visiting

valley

vine

violet

viper

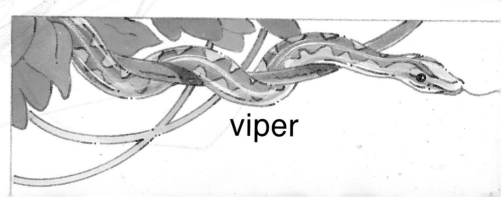

n o p q r s t u v w x y z

unpacking

vest

umbrella

under

village

volcano

van

a b c d e f g h i j k l m

whale

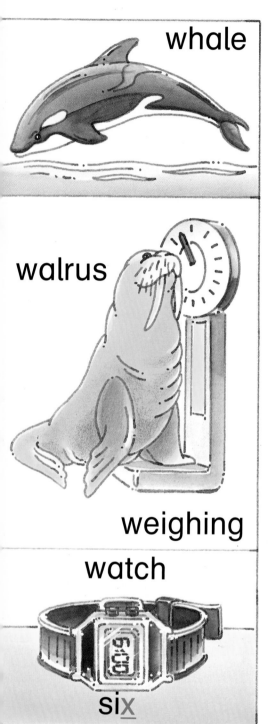

walrus

weighing

watch

six

wood

window   wall

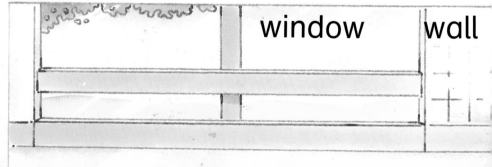

n o p q r s t u v **w x y** z

water wing

wave

water

woodpecker

relaxing

box

a b c d e f g h i j k l m

zebra

yo-yo

yeast

zigzag

zero

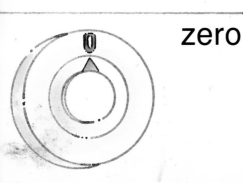

zip

yolk

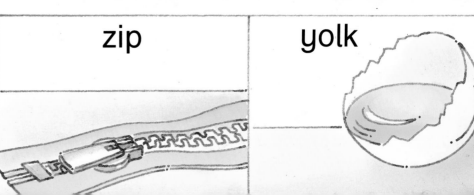

n o p q r s t u v w x y z

yak

yawning

bu**zz**ing

yam

yucca

yoghurt

yellow